Ernie

An Autobiography of Ernest Bontrager

Ernie Publications
P. O. Box 50125
Sarasota, Fl. 34232
(941) 724-4125

Ernie

An Autobiography of Ernest Bontrager

Published by Ernie Publications

©2001 by Ernest Bontrager

Cover Pictures are as follows:
Mark and Mike Bontrager are our 2 adopted boys.
Amish Boy-Myself in 1st grade.
Horse and buggies taken in Arthur Illinois, at a funeral.
World Trade Center, New York
Lied Transplant Center, Omaha Nebraska

Scripture quotations are from:
The Holy Bible, King James Version (KJV)

For information
Ernie Publications
P. O. Box 50125
Sarasota, Fl. 34232
(941) 724-4125

Quantity discounts for churches and schools.

ISBN 0-9716810-0-7 (soft cover)

Acknowledgements
Heartfelt thanks to my editors: Rose & Candace Milan, Ray & Ella Bontrager.
I appreciate all of you.

Ernie

Contents

In The Beginning

In the beginning God created the heaven and the earth.

Genesis 1:1

Amish Boyhood

Knock, knock! Hey John. There's someone at the front door. Now, who is it this time? It was just four days after Christmas on December 29th. John gets out of bed, and goes to the front door. There is his Amish neighbor Ray, standing at the front door. Could you please take us to the hospital? My wife is expecting. John said, "Sure." Wait just a minute and let me get some clothes on. John gets his car out and picks up Ella, and takes them to the hospital. This is the beginning of Ernie, who was born in 1951.

This chapter is about the beginning of my Amish boyhood. I was joined in this life by a brother, Willie, who was almost 2 years older than I. We were born to an Amish family in central Illinois. Of course I do not remember too much about what happened next, but they told me I used to wear a dress. I wasn't very happy about that. But I did not have too much to say about it. When I was around age five, there was an outbreak of polio among the Amish. We do not hear much about that any more but several of the Amish young people did get polio, and they thought I was going to get it. In fact several times I had a fever of 105. Of course, we did not have a car and in the evening Dad would put me in the buggy, and take me to the doctor. The doctor would tell my Dad, "Why do you wait so long before you bring him in?" Anyway, I survived that summer and did not get polio.

About a year later, before they had a lot of modern equipment, my Dad and Mom were out shucking corn by hand. My brother was about eight at the time. He was driving a team of horses and pulling a wagon. It was one of these big old steel wheeled wagons, about half full of ear corn. I was sitting up on the seat with my brother, Willie. All of a sudden one of the ears of corn missed the wagon. I thought I could help out here. I crawled off of the wagon and retrieved this ear of corn. Just then it was time to move forward. My brother said giddy-up and the team pulled forward, and the back wheel of the wagon went right over my back. They thought sure; I was going to have something wrong with me. But the dirt was soft enough, that it just pushed me down into it. Of course I was hurting for a while, but I probably cried. They say children cry sometimes; but big men do not cry. I am 6'2" and 280 pounds now. I have cried more in the last 3 months than I did as a child.

Soon after the accident, I started going to school. I went to the Yoder School. Which is right close to Grandpa Miller's place. It was a one-room schoolhouse. They had all eight grades. I only went there about half a year. One thing I remember, and I still have trouble with it sometimes, is doing math. I kept getting all my math questions wrong and the teacher could not figure out what was going on. In front of the whole class she got a box of little tacks and I had to count these out one at a time. And so I started counting seven, eight, nine, ten, eleven, --, thirteen, fourteen, fifteen and I kept missing one number. And she said, "Uh-oh, there is your problem." So after that, I started adding and subtracting, and it worked a little better.

At age seven we moved to Grandpa Miller's place. This was back in 1958. At the same time, there was an opportunity to rent land over in Sullivan, which was on the western edge of the Amish community. Dad decided to check it out and decided to move there. There were several families at that time that decided to start a new church. This was called the Pleasant View Church. It was built back in 1958-1959.

As Amish we had no running hot water unless mom got in a hurry. We would take a bath on Saturday night, in a little washtub, in the living room. Mom would heat the water on the stove. We would take a bath once a week, if we needed it or not. Then of course we did not have electricity, or a telephone. I think at that time we did have a bathroom inside, but most people didn't. We had gas operated lights, refrigerator and stove.

After we moved to Sullivan we had electricity, a telephone, and a car.

I remember when we left the Amish my Dad bought a black 1954 Chevy. Boy! We thought we had it made. Now this thing was just so nice and shiny. I still remember when he pulled up that night. I was up stairs in the bedroom. I looked out and saw this shiny car come in, and just couldn't wait to get a ride in it.

Then we moved to Sullivan. In the first few years my dad worked in the sale barn. If we got to go along that was a big event in our lives. Especially if we got to go to the cafeteria, where they had hamburgers, hotdogs and soda pop. That was such a treat. We just could not imagine how we could have it any better than that.

My Mom's sister had several boys our age that we would spend time with. Cousins, Larry and Glen were quite adventurous young men and when Mom and Dad went to a wedding, funeral, or had to leave town for something, we would stay with them. We had lots of fun with them. They built a wooden raft and mounted an engine on it, and cut open a 55-

gallon barrel, to make a paddle wheel for propulsion. They lined the outside of the wooden raft with more barrels and we launched it into the pond on their place. We went out fishing and jumping off this thing, we certainly had a great time. We almost drowned when the 55 gallon barrels filled up with water.

One time cousin Larry was driving their propane fueled 3010 John Deere tractor, and my brother Willis and I, were sitting on the fenders. I was sitting on the right fender.

Larry decided to take out their brand new tractor and show us how to mow the roadsides. I was sitting on the side of the sickle mower. All of a sudden he slammed on the brakes and they really hold on a 3010. I flew off into the mower and landed on the other side of the bar. He turned it off really quick. I don't think we ever told our parents about it.

About a year later or so, we had a big semi come into our place. They unloaded two brand new tractors. A 3010 and a 4010. Man I thought we had it made. We always did like John Deere. I guess the color green is still in our blood. We just had a great time, at Sullivan.

I attended public school. The school bus would come each day. I remember one time, I ran behind the school bus, instead of walking around to the front. The driver got pretty upset with me. I was always very shy. I was in second grade and I always wore my Amish hat. I was still pretty Amish at that time. Nobody else in the whole school was Amish. I really developed an inferiority complex and was very shy. I still am, for that matter. But I did like books. I like to read. Since we did not have radio or TV, there wasn't much entertainment other than books. They called me a bookworm. I was only allowed to check out 2 books from the school library each day. I would read my sister Marie's books also. At school we would always have the chance on Fridays to give a book report. One time I was so sick that I couldn't go to school. My Mom took me in just for the book report, because I didn't want to miss one book report the whole year, which I didn't. Then my teacher told me something that I just didn't understand at that time, but she said "You have the best mother in the world." Looking back now, I can agree with that 100%. I had a lot of fun playing there in Sullivan. We lived in a small tenant house. The landlord moved into town and retired. We got the chance to live in the big house. The big house was full of antiques, a wind up record player, and in the garage there was a Model-T. We just had more fun playing and sitting in the Model-T; just dreaming about the time we could have our own car, and be out in real life.

At this time I would like to give a little history about the differences between Amish, Beachy and Mennonite. When I was born, I was Amish; we had a horse and buggy, and lived in the heart of the Amish community in Central Illinois. There are other communities, Pennsylvania, Indiana, and Ohio. In fact, there are Amish in all 50 states. The Mennonites were named after Menno Simon and then later Jacob Amman started the Amish. There are different types of Amish as far as their beliefs, but they are all hard working people. They just have a real good heart, as far as their work attitudes, and so forth. It has become quite commercialized in some areas. Tourists come to enjoy the furniture and quilts they make, and of course the fine food they prepare. Mose Beachy started the Beachy church. This group was a little more liberal than the Amish but more conservative than the Mennonites. They have cars, and a lot of them were farmers and needed to be a little more competitive in the market place. They needed to be able to use modern machinery. Otherwise they could not compete with other farmers in the area. Mennonites are also in all 50 states, and are all over the world for that matter.

In this chapter we are talking about God's creation. There is only one heaven, and whether you are Amish, Beachy, or Mennonite, or whatever your religion, it will not get you into heaven alone. You must be 100% committed to Jesus Christ. To enter into the gates of glory, the choice is yours. That's what I am trying to do with this book. Help each one, as they grow older, that they could understand, that God created the universe. He created each one of us uniquely and different. He knows what each one of us needs, and I just want to help you, to not make the same mistakes that I did.

As I grew older, I continued to be fascinated with equipment, and I have built my own go-kart. I didn't have anything to build it with, and had to rob parts off the farm equipment. I found four good wheels and an engine off a tiller. It was a big red Briggs & Stratton, 8 horsepower engine. I welded the frame together and put a steering wheel on it. I took off down the road. Of course I made a U- turn, and as I turned, a little bit too fast, the thing fell over and dumped me off into a ditch, and the go-kart was sitting on top of me. That sort of ended that career. Also later, I built a couple of high-wheel bicycles. I just turned the bicycle up side down and added 3 foot to the handlebars and seat, and turned the pedals around, and hey, the circus was in town.

At the ripe old age of 16, I got my first car. A 1966 black Plymouth Valient slant 6, 3-speed tranny, with red interior. WOW!!! That was quite a hot rod. It was a hand me down, because my brother had pretty much used it up, before I got it.

After quitting school I worked on the farm part time. I also worked as an electrician and learned how to wire a house. I also worked at a pallet shop, and the owner was Amish. He did not have any electricity in the shop. Everything was powered by diesel engines connected to a drive shaft. Also compressed air and hydraulics were used to control saws and nailers. He needed a machine to drill multiple holes in plywood so I designed and built a machine that could drill up to 8 holes at one time. The spindles were adjustable and an air motor drove it all.

I attended the Pleasant View Church and went to Bible school, and met a lot of other young folks, but never took Christianity to heart. I never tried to win someone else, to Christ. I think we can all look back now, and wish things would be different.

I never graduated from high school, and dropped out at tenth grade. Don't do that! Ignorance is swift to speak!

Howard, Andy & Ernie were the special music trio in our church. We would sing acapella hymns on Sunday evening. Howard is now the Bishop or senior pastor, at the church along with Willie, my older brother. As teenagers we would go to Howard's place on Sunday afternoon and play basketball in their hayloft. Andy would play his guitar, and sing every Buck Owens song he knew.

Each year as teenager's we would go to different states in the summer for Youth Fellowship Meetings. When I was sixteen we had it here in Illinois. I was asked to have devotions and I couldn't get the butterflies to fly in rotation. My knees shook so bad the noise was deafening. At seventeen we went to Kansas and I remember after dark we piled onto the back of pickup trucks and went chasing jackrabbits. We used a spot light and those red eyes looked eerily at us and as we got closer, they would hop away. They could really move fast.

Howard married a lady from Iowa; Andy married a gal also from Iowa, and I found one from Ohio. But that is another story.

Everything in this book is true, and I hope that you can learn from my mistakes, and get it right the first time. I had every chance and knew the Bible better than most people. I remember coming home from Bible school in Arkansas, and by then I had a real car. A 1965 Dodge Saturn, green with gold flex paint---- Oh nooooo, Dad had it painted black! At that time we could have any color car, as long as it was black. Sounds just like Henry Ford.

When we were coming home from Arkansas we stopped and bought some fireworks. Gary was driving one car and I was following him.

We were going over a bridge in Cairo Illinois, and Darrell couldn't wait till we got home, and decided to start the show. He would light a firecracker, and throw it out the window. Well the wind blew it back in the open window, and it landed in the paper sack. All of a sudden, I saw smoke billowing out of the car, and the driver had his head out of the window, so he could see. Seems like a smoke bomb caught on fire as, the whole paper bag of fireworks started to go off. The police were sitting on the other end of the bridge, and stared in amazement as these wild teenagers, kept going past them. We did not dare stop, and they finally stomped out the fireworks and threw the bag out. I think their ears must still be ringing today!

Wandering in the Wilderness

Now therefore if ye will obey my voice indeed, and keep my covenant, then ye shall be a peculiar treasure unto me above all people: for all the earth is mine.
                                                                Exodus 19:5

Life Of Modern Man

In 1971 the Vietnam war was going no place. As a Christian, we were allowed to do a two year volunteer service, instead of going to the Army. We practice non-resistance, and feel that it is wrong, to take another one's life.

I just followed the footsteps of my older brother, and worked at a nursing home, in Florida. I served as an orderly the first year, and then worked in the laundry the second year. Every Tuesday evening, we played volleyball, and at 6'2" I loved to be in the front row. If the ball would be set up right, I could score with a slam dunk, every time.

We stayed in dorms, and had all our food provided. The first 6 months, we were paid $35.00 a month, and the next 18, got a whopping $124.00 a month. I would keep track of every penny I spent, and had money left over, each month. I was always looking for ways to supplement my income and did some lawn work on Siesta Key. Also, Leroy had a garage in Pinecraft, and I would change water pumps, alternators, and work on VW motors, in my spare time.

Orpha, one of the nurses, had an eight-track player in her car and she would bring me records and cassettes of music she would like recorded, on eight-track. I would buy blank-eight track tapes, and purchased an eight-track recorder. Then I

9

would charge her $20 per tape, for the recording fee. In an electronics catalog, I found this 200-watt amplifier kit that was really a sweet deal. I was working night duty, at the time. At the nurses station, I plugged in my soldering iron, and put this amp together. Next I bought some speakers, and had Sheldon, who worked at a cabinet shop, make me some speaker cabinets, and finished them with Formica. My room was the most popular one in the boy's dorm, because the music would rattle the walls.

Another way to make money in our spare time was to help mow the grass. It almost cost me my life! The nursing home had a 318 John Deere riding lawnmower, with a grass catcher on the back. I was mowing the front lawn one morning, and the grass was too wet. The chute from the grass catcher kept plugging up, and I would stop to unplug it. One time I forgot to turn off the mower blades, and as I reached in with my right hand, it almost took off my finger. I went to the hospital and waited 4 hours, for them to sew my finger back together. A few days later I got very sick, and spent 4 days in the hospital with staph infection. I was a jack-of-all-trades. The nursing home decided to buy a grandfather clock from the Howard Miller Co. It came in kit form. I glued, sawed, and worked for 3 weeks, putting it together. The guests really enjoyed listening to the chimes and the tick-tocks.

I met Sarah while working at the home and got married on June 23, 1973. We lived in Pinecraft, rent-free for the 1st 6 months, at a friend's house. We then moved out in the country on a 7-acre tract of land. We lived in the back, in a one-room apartment. Sarah would clean the big house, and I would mow the lawn and pick up the trash from over 100 palm trees. They called the place "Falling Fronds" because after every wind storm there were branches everywhere. We lived there for 2 years rent-free. I would ride my 350 Honda motorcycle to work at Skyline Mobile Homes. For the first 2 years I worked in the cabinet department, building base cabinets. The next 3 years I was foreman over the cabinet and mill departments, and had 8-10 men working for me. As supervisor I was responsible for repairs and would have to go into the doublewide homes, out in the yard. You can imagine how hot these homes were in the Florida sun. I would open the door and get hit by a blast of formaldehyde, oozing from the paneling. Mix that with the paint, glue, and carpet smells. My eyes would sting and I could hardly breath. I think maybe that is when my liver started to go bad. It was from the chemical exposure. One of the jobs of the liver is to remove the toxins from the body.

We saved up $4,000 and bought a vacant lot in Sarasota Springs, and in 1976 built a new 3 bedroom, 2 bath room, house.

I started to read real estate books and bought my first 4 – unit apartment building in 1977. I started to watch the newspaper for apartments for sale and came across a package deal. A 28 unit 2 story building and 2 houses close by. I borrowed $5,000.00 on a credit card and took over the mortgages, and they were ours. I worked on every apartment and raised the rents from $150.00 month to over $200.00 month. I gradually got better tenants and would spend a lot of time in the courthouse, writing up eviction notices. It takes a strong stomach sometimes, to clean up the messes they leave. I found a loaded gun in one apartment. It is lucky I didn't get shot.

If you think it takes money to make money you just aren't trying. A positive attitude and determination is all it takes. Most people like to live in their comfort zone. It is hard for them to make a decision. I think it is better to make the wrong decision, than to not make any at all. Those were pretty good years. I hired a manager to collect rents and do minor repairs. We would stop in every Friday evening and pick up the rent money. This property today, is worth over 2 million dollars. But as you will see later everything falls apart. If God is not with you all is in vain. God was trying to talk to us, but we were too busy to listen. I got bored with the apartments, and went to real estate school, and eventually got my Florida Real Estate Broker's License. Wow! Seems everyone in Florida got theirs' too. I worked with Abe at Cypress Realty and sold enough real estate, to make minimum wage. Then in the 1980's interest rates went to 18 percent and selling real estate, was like selling refrigerators to the Eskimos!

Since I was an electronics nut, I bought my first computer from Radio Shack. It had 16K of ram, a keyboard and used a cassette recorder for storage. You could buy plug in cartridges, and play games in color. I would show my friends and family how it worked, and they would laugh at me, because they said they would never be able to learn to use something like that. Now they all have computers with e-mail, and know more about computers than I do! Since real estate was slow, I decided to start selling computers and software and servicing computers. Before the Internet and e-mail, there was a thing called BBS. Bulletin Board Service. If you knew the BBS phone number you could connect two computers together with a modem and do primitive e-mail. I operated the first Color BBS in Sarasota in 1981. I named my store Family Computers. We sold Sanyo and Commodore Amiga computers. The computer store and Real Estate office, were in the same building. I had a lot of fun running the business, but decided to sell it after an unfortunate incident at the office. The real estate broker that I was working for ran into financial difficulty. One Monday morning as I arrived at the store, the real estate secretary said, "Don't go in there." I called my pastor. After the coroner was there, they took him away. I was very distraught, and could not understand how such a respected person, could take his own life. I got out of real estate sales and sold the computer store, to one of my employees.

My wife developed thyroid problems and we decided to sell the apartments in 1989. After 10 years of ownership we got just enough at closing to pay off what we owed on the mortgage, and were getting $2000.00 a month profit. We bought a 5-acre parcel in the country, and started planning our dream home. But God had other plans. We had $600.00 month coming in from the computer store, and then the economy went south and he filed for bankruptcy. Instead of paying $400.00 month store rent, he moved the store to a strip mall, and was paying over $2,000.00 month rent. So we kissed the $600.00 a month good bye, and lost $20,000.00 in equity. So I bought a lawn mower and started mowing lawns. That is O.K. in the winter, but is a lot of work in the summer. I also started hauling trash from contractors' job sites, and after 2 years sold the lawn business part. I then bought a trailer and Bobcat skid steer loader, and went full time into demolition and trash pickup. The guy who bought our apartments took a stupid pill, and went to Orlando and bought another 100-unit apartment building. Real estate values in the early 80's took a nose-dive. With the Savings & Loan Crisis he could not borrow money, and ended up filing for bankruptcy also. We could not collect on our judgment of over $500,000.00, and ended up selling our land in the country.

So now what? Our dreams were shattered. I was very depressed and felt like such a failure. I think that happens to everybody. It is how we react to our negative circumstances. That makes a difference. If life gives us lemons, make lemonade. I sure wish my kidneys would understand that. Ha! See chapter 4. I always thought that if everything else goes bad I could always work and get back on track. So at the ripe old age of 49, after 9 years of innocence as a Amish boy, and 40 years of wandering around, with no direction in life, I was at the end of myself. I was facing my biggest challenge yet.

I was just like the children of Israel, who wandered in the wilderness for 40 years. They were discontented with all that God had done for them. How easily we forget the blessings we have in our life. The very situations that cause most people to become discouraged and bitter are allowed by God to teach us. We need to realize our need for him and his power in our lives. It is only by the power of God, that we will be able to achieve genuine love and respond to each trial in a positive way.

- Thank God for all things-even trials.
- Rejoicing in all things by finding benefits in them.
- Doing good works for all people-even our enemies.

To the degree we carry out these responses, we will experience the power of genuine love.

Because of the disobedience of the Israelites they were denied access to the Promised Land.

The Day The World Stood Still

Yea though I walk through the valley of the shadow of death, I will fear no evil: for thou art with me; thy rod and thy staff comfort me.
Psalm 23:4

9-11

Just as Pearl Harbor stands out in American history, we will all remember that awful day. Terrorist attacks shake the nation and world. 9-11-01 Tuesday, September 11, 2001.

The worst terrorist attack in U.S. history killed thousands, and destroyed the World Trade Center in New York, damaged the Pentagon and shook financial markets and businesses around the world. And the shock waves continued overnight as Asian markets dropped dramatically while the human cost and economic damage was still being assessed.

The crash of four hijacked U.S. airliners led to the unprecedented grounding of all commercial flights in the United States through at least noon Wednesday and led to the closing of U.S. financial markets for a second day Wednesday. Concern that the attack would shake consumer confidence and plunge an already shaky U.S. economy into recession sent stocks plunging Tuesday in Europe, led by financial and insurance issues. Stocks fell sharply elsewhere in the Americas as well. Major Asian markets, including Japan's Nikkei, plummeted when delayed trading started there about 8:30 p.m. ET Tuesday.

The second World Trade Center tower collapses after Tuesday's terrorist attack. The confidence of investors in the stability of U.S. markets is very important said Edward Leamer, a professor of business finance at the UCLA Anderson School of Management. "The U.S. had the image of being a safe harbor for investors," he said. "This may have a psychological impact on global investors who make take this moment in history to reassess their positions." U.S. financial officials, including Treasury Secretary Paul O'Neill, expressed confidence in the strength of U.S. markets. The Federal Reserve issued a statement Tuesday that it is making money available to banks to insure liquidity in the system.

Officials with Afghanistan's government are suspected of supporting fugitive Saudi accused terrorist Osama bin Laden, whom U. S. officials believe may be involved in Tuesday's attacks, although Afghan officials made a statement condemning the attacks.

Businesses, schools and public offices around the nation closed in response to the attacks. Many U.S. and European financial services companies had offices in the destroyed World Trade Center, and the firms were scrambling Tuesday to determine the status of their employees and find locations for survivors to return to work.

Gold and oil prices spiked soon after the attacks while the dollar fell in overseas markets. European stock markets saw stock prices plunge. Most major businesses throughout the nation's financial center closed early Tuesday, and limited access to and from the city made the prospects for normal operations Wednesday doubtful as well. The impact of the attack was also felt across the nation as many major businesses and factories, including the nation's major automakers, also closed as a precaution.

The nation's struggling airline industry appeared poised to take a huge hit in the coming weeks and months. Air travel has fallen sharply after previous high-profile terrorism, such as the crash of the Pan Am flight over Lockerbie, Scotland in 1988, and also after the Iraqi invasion of Kuwait in 1990. Air travel was already off sharply due to the slowing of the U.S. economy.

No information on deaths from the attacks was immediately available, but the toll is certain to be high. The attacks hit just as the New York workday began, when the buildings were filling with people. The towers have about 50,000 employees and 100,000 visitors on a typical day, according to some estimates. The collapse of the structures showered the streets below with tons of debris. Still many employees of the center were able to escape relatively unscathed in the time between the crash and the collapse of the building. Matthew Cornelous, an employee of the agency that runs the New York area airports, was at work on the 65th floor of the Trade Center when the crash occurred. He said he and many other people were able to get out of the building through the staircases. "Every one maintained calm really well—I was impressed with that," Cornelous told CNN. "We didn't understand the full severity of the situation, so people weren't panicking. We never had any fear of the building collapse.
"For some people it brought back memories of the bombing," he said, referring to the 1993 terrorist blast that emptied the towers but caused relatively few casualties. "People had been there before," he said. The first jet to crash apparently was American Airlines Flight 11, a Boeing 767 en route from Boston to Los Angeles with 81 passengers, nine flight attendants and two pilots that American confirmed had been lost in a "tragic accident." Next apparently was United Airlines flight 175, a Boeing 767 bound from Boston to Los Angeles with 56 passengers, two pilots, and seven flight attendants. It

apparently was crashed into Tower Two, causing an explosion on the far side of the tower. United Flight 93, a Boeing 757 flying from Newark, N.J., to San Francisco, apparently crashed near Pittsburgh with 38 passengers, two pilots and five flight attendants aboard. Finally, American also confirmed that its flight 77 from Washington Dulles Airport to Los Angeles had crashed. It apparently was used in the attack on the Pentagon. It carried 58 passengers, four flight attendants and two pilots. Following that attack, the Pentagon burst into flames and a part of one side of the five-sided structure collapsed. Secondary explosions were reported in the aftermath of the attack and smoke billowed skyward toward the Potomac River and the city beyond.

President Bush was in Sarasota, Fla., at the time of the attack, and called the attacks a national tragedy. "Terrorism against our nation will not stand," Bush said. The president immediately left Sarasota but due to security concerns he went to an undisclosed location rather than return to Washington.

He issued a further statement saying all resources of the federal government will be put into catching those responsible, and helping victims of the attack. The government has taken security precautions and U.S. military forces around the world were on high alert status, he added.

"The United States will hunt down and punish those responsible for these cowardly attacks," he said. "The resolve of our great nation is being tested. Make no mistake, we will show the world we will pass the test."

The past three summers I was living in Illinois. Florida was too hot for me because my liver disease was getting worse. I was diagnosed with PSC (Primary Schlerosing Cholingitis). This is a gradually degrading disease and causes cirrhosis and is terminal. I kept going to different doctors and was misdiagnosed for many years. In January of 1996 Dr. Birkner in Sarasota gave me the proper diagnosis. He told me I have two years to live and that there is no cure except for having a liver transplant. That evening I found out that my health insurance will not pay for a liver transplant. I was told that the cost would be about $300,000.00 Insurance is just like wearing a hospital gown. You are just not as well covered as you think you are!

Did you ever have a bad day? Did you ever feel like giving up? I said "Lord, what's coming next?"

We need to be like Paul and seek God's strength in our weakness. 2 Corinthians 12: 9, 10 And he said unto me, My grace is sufficient for thee: for my strength is made perfect in weakness. Most gladly therefore will I rather glory in my infirmities, that the power of Christ may rest upon me. Therefore I take pleasure in infirmities, in reproaches, in necessities, in persecutions, in distresses for Christ's sake: for when I am weak, then am I strong.

My doctor told me to go to Omaha Nebraska for an evaluation and then get listed for a transplant. In February we went to the University of Nebraska Medical Center and were listed for transplant in July of 1996. So for the next 5 years I was waiting for an O negative blood type donor that weighed 270 pounds. There is a shortage of organs for transplantation. Thousands of people die every year because of the shortage of organs. More than 79,0000 people in the past year were on a waiting list for a donor organ. In addition, hundreds of thousands of patients can benefit from the use of donor bone, cornea, tendons and other tissues.

How do I sign up to be an organ and/or tissue donor? Sign the back of your driver's license at any time, (not just when renewing your license). Most importantly, discuss your wishes with your family because they must give final consent for donation to take place, so it is very important they know how you feel about donation.

Who may be eligible to be an organ and/or tissue donor? Almost anyone, from newborn to senior citizen. A person's ability to donate may be affected by a number of factors that will be assessed at the time of death.

What is brain death?

Brain death occurs when blood and the oxygen it carries cannot flow to the brain. Without blood and oxygen, the brain dies. When the brain dies, the person cannot move, breathe, think or feel. Pain and suffering ceases. The heart can continue to beat for a while as the ventilator (breathing machine) provides artificial support and oxygen to the body. It may look like the person is sleeping because the ventilator fills the lungs with oxygen and helps keep the skin pink and warm. They are not sleeping. Brain death is death and cannot be reversed.

What is the difference between an organ and a tissue?

Organs are heart, lungs, liver, kidneys, pancreas and small bowel and can be donated only when a patient is still on artificial support at time of death. Tissues include eyes, fascia, lata, bone, heart valves, saphenous veins, skin and tendons and can be donated either off or on artificial support at time of death.

Will donation affect the appearance of the donor?

No. Donation does not alter the ability to have an open-casket funeral.

Does my religion permit me to donate my organs and/or tissues? All major religions have endorsed organ and tissue donation and transplantation as a means to help others.

Amish: If a transplant is needed for the well being of an individual, the Amish will consent to the transplantation. According to John Hostetler, Amish religion and professor of anthropology at Temple University in Philadelphia, "The Amish believe that since God created the human body, it is God who heals. However, nothing in the Amish understanding of the Bible forbids them from using modern medical services, including surgery, hospitalization, dental work, anesthesia, blood transfusions or immunization."

Mennonite: Mennonites have no formal position on donation, but they are not opposed to it. They believe the decision to donate is up to the individual and/or his or her family.

At 45 years of age I wasn't about to give up. I put together some people from various churches in Florida and started to do some fundraising. I tried to get health insurance but was told that they would not cover any pre-existing conditions. After some effort I found out about a new law in Florida, that if you own a business you can get a group plan that has full coverage. The first company pulled out of Florida and canceled me on June 30, 1998. I was jaundiced and went to the hospital on July 14th for 4 days. $11,000.00 later and no insurance! I was able to get a new policy within the 60-day time limit and finally had health coverage again.

I sold the Bobcat business to two brothers from Michigan. By this time I had 3 trucks and a new Bobcat. I was working in the Florida heat and that summer I started to get a fever and would get very nauseous. We were always hauling trash to the landfill and I got tired of getting out of the truck to open the tailgate. Slopping through the mud and garbage and dodging sea gulls was no fun. I designed and patented a tailgate that would automatically open as the dump bed was raised. I kept this truck and Mike my 21 year old uses it now to haul away concrete roof tiles.

Since I was having more and more difficulty working, I decided to spend the summers in Illinois and 4 months in Florida at wintertime. I was always wearing a sweater in the air conditioning and was always cold. My liver could not control my body temperature and the chills and fevers were a frequent occurrence.

I attended the Pleasant View Church where I attended before I moved to Florida some 30 years ago. It was good to come back home and spend time with my family. I had two brothers, three sisters, all their children and of course mom and dad.

My brother Willis and family spent 3 years in Romania serving at the orphanage in Suceava. He was a minister at the local church and was in charge of teaching the native pastors and the youth. My parents and I had a chance to go over and visit for several weeks and were amazed at the culture shock. Bucharest was a modern city much like in America. The countryside was very primitive and people used horses and even oxen to pull their carts down the road. The mission work was funded by CAM. We got to go along to help distribute food parcels to the poor. They have a dairy and supply milk for several orphanages. They raise corn and other grains that are used for distribution to the poor. Another interesting work is the teaching of the native women how to sew. They have several sewing rooms stocked with donated material and sewing machines. There is a real shortage of affordable clothes and shoes. It seems a lot of time was spent in gathering firewood and just surviving from day to day.

Getting back to the states, I needed to find something to do so I could earn some money to pay for all the expenses of going to Omaha several times each year. I was on low priority classification on the list and kept waiting for the call but it never came.

I borrowed a semi-tractor and trailer from my brother-in-law, and passed my CDL (Commercial Drivers License) and started hauling grain part time the first year. We would take corn and soybeans from the local elevator to ADM where they processed it into corn sweetener and ethanol. The beans were cooked (Pugh!) and made into meal and many other products.

The next 2 summers I started to make trips to Michigan 2 to 3 times a week. I pulled a 53' long trailer and it was 13'6" tall. Sometimes I would pick-up loads in downtown Chicago and the clearance on the "L" (elevated trains) overpass was less than 12'. On one of my trips to Grand Rapids I went to a woodworking show. I was fascinated with a computerized laser machine that would engrave and cut wood with a beam of light. Since I had some computer experience, I decided to buy one and started Extreme Laser Works. I knew that I would not be able to go back to driving truck after the transplant and thought this might be a good way to keep busy while recovering. The first summer I had the machine set up in the same school building in Sullivan, where I attended grade school. The Yoder's transformed the building into the Old School Market. Each room is filled with crafts and Amish furniture. They also have a buffet that serves great Amish food. I would drive truck during the week and spend Friday and Saturday running the retail laser business. I learned a lot about all the different capabilities of the laser. Not only engraving on wood but leather, acrylic, coated metals, plastic signs, marble, Brazilian Agate, and plaques. To view some samples of our work, go to extremelaserworks.com.

This past summer of 2001, I was supposed to go to Omaha in July for a checkup, but decided I needed a vacation first. So I bought a 3-day vacation package in June and planned to go to Branson Missouri in August. I asked for time off and was all set to have a good time playing instead of listening to the doctor. Why is it that we are always putting off the important things in life? I think we are all a little bit self centered and selfish. In order to use the vacation package I had to mail it in 3 weeks in advance. Guess what? I waited and waited and it got lost in the mail. In over 10 years of ordering products, I had never lost an order in the mail. So I canceled the first order and ordered another one, but it got delivered too late to use it in August. So I went to Omaha in August instead of going to Branson. I did not know what God had in store for me but there was a reason for the lost mail.

After doing a blood test the doctor said we have to do more tests. He was very concerned about developing cancer in the bile ducts. The cirrhosis was much worse and they moved me to 2B priority on the waiting list. Now I am on medium priority and have a much better chance of getting transplanted. I was very anemic and had trouble concentrating. I would get nosebleeds that I could not stop. Since the bile ducts were clogged up the bile would stay in the blood and cause my skin to itch. I was so miserable the last couple of years that it became almost unbearable.

While at the hospital I had the chance to attend a group meeting that consisted of people that are waiting, or have already had liver transplants. They mentioned that there was a group of pilots in the Midwest that would donate their plane and would fly patients to the hospital for free. The name of the organization is Air Life Line Midwest. They are based in Peoria Illinois. 1-800-822-7972 We were told that we needed to be in Omaha in 4 hours from the time we received the call. Well, it is 8-9 hours driving time and so we applied for a wallet card so we could get the plane service when needed. The cards came on Monday the 10th of September. My last day of trucking was on the 11th and I listened to the events of the day on the radio. (9-11) We had scheduled our Branson trip on the 12th and planned to leave at 6 A.M. At 4 A.M. Joyce the transplant coordinator called and wanted to know if we could get to Omaha as a backup for a liver transplant. Because there were no planes flying we told her that we could not get there in time. Later we found out that the other person did make it in time and got the transplant. After much debate, my parents and Mom's sister and myself headed out on vacation. We had a great time and on Thursday went to Eurcka Springs Arkansas and took the Holy Land Tour. We visited a tabernacle and were guided by an old Messianic Jew and he explained the Old Testament rituals. We walked by the Sea of Galilee with Peter and saw the replica of the tomb where Jesus lay. In the evening we watched the Passion play that depicted the last 2 weeks of Jesus' life on earth.

On Friday morning the 14th, Omaha called again at 4 A. M. Since we were closer we told them we would be there in 4 hours. Wow! What a shock, two calls in one week. I called ahead on the cell phone and arranged for a plane to pick up Dad and myself at Kansas City, Missouri. As we traveled on the interstate at daybreak I looked up in the clouds. In the eastern sky we all saw the empty cross. I took it to mean that Jesus was watching over us. A reminder of the ascension we saw depicted at the Passion play, the night before. Halleluiah! He is risen indeed. We flew to Omaha, and Mom and Sovilla drove the van on into Omaha. One brother and 2 sisters drove out to Omaha from Illinois. After a flurry of activity, I was being prepped for surgery when one of the surgeons came out and said the donor liver was no good. My family was upset, but I was a happy camper. I was nervous all day and just was not ready. I let fear rule my heart. We all stayed the night and the next morning I said, " Let's go home." I finally called the nurse coordinator and asked what we should do. She said it might be another month or year before we would get a call. We went back home on Saturday. In church the next day I was asked by Wesley to lead a song but did not feel like singing. Instead I asked the church to continue praying for me, not knowing that the next evening I would be called again.

These things have I spoken unto you, that in me ye might have peace. In the world ye shall have tribulation: but be of good cheer; I have overcome the World. John 16:33

So in less than one week, after waiting for over 4 years, I was called 3 times. The waiting and not knowing was the hardest part of the whole process. I would wake up at night in a cold sweat, just convinced that today would definitely be the day. I prayed that God would send a sign before the call and I was sure that somehow I would recognize when the time was approaching.

Now back to 9-11. Because of the lack of airplane service and long security checks, flying commercial was too time consuming. The hospital started calling people that could get there sooner. That is why I got 3 calls in such a short time. Remember, there were 3 planes that crashed into buildings and caused a lot of damage. Was God giving me a sign? But what about the 4th airplane?

Rebirth

And be renewed in the spirit of your mind;
and that ye put on the new man, which after God
has created in righteousness and true holiness.

Ephesians 4: 23-24

My Liver Transplant

It was Monday September 17th, 2001. I had to go to work at midnight. So I did bookkeeping in the morning and finished up some laser orders in the afternoon. Mom and Dad had a Haiti board meeting that night. So I went to Mattoon and bought some clothes and ate at the Cracker Barrel restaurant. I talked to Mom and Dad for ten minutes when they came home from the meeting. I then left for work about 11:00 p.m. At 11:05 p.m. the phone rang. It was Omaha. I was at work and was just getting into my truck to leave for Michigan. Glen was changing oil in my Kenworth tractor and we were talking about the schedule for that week. Then Eloise, his wife, came running out and said, "Omaha called, Ernie, call your Dad". I said to her "What do they want now?" Da, What do you think they wanted? I raced back home.

We drove to Bloomington, Illinois in less than one hour. It would normally take 1½ hours. We met the pilot at the airport. Dad and I climbed on board a 1 million dollar, twin turbo prop plane to Omaha, NE. The pilot was a flight instructor and was on the board of Air Life Line Midwest. We arrived at 3:15 a.m. I went into surgery at 11:30 a.m. on Tuesday, September 18, 2001, and I was in the operating room for eight hours. The next morning the tubes were out and I was alert by 9:30 a.m. The next day the 20th of September, I was moved to the seventh floor in the Special Liver Transplant Section. On Friday the 21st, all tubes were off. In the evening I was walking the halls. I had an upside down smile on my belly with 49 staples to hold the incision closed. I am 49 years old.

On Saturday the doctor said I could go to cooperative care, but I had company coming and I said I would rather wait till Monday. On Sunday Darryls' and Dans' were there along with Mom and Dad. We had church in our room. The nurses said, "It sounded like angels were singing." We have met many other patients and one that I remember that we encountered was Terry Nelson who was only 34 years old. He had Cancer and needed a liver transplant, but because of Cancer he could not get on the list. He had the same disease that I had, but was misdiagnosed for many years.

Every day 7 potential liver transplant patients die in the hospital because of the liver organ donor shortage. I have list of web sites listed in the back of the book, if you would like more information.

Another purpose in writing this book is to educate the public, that by being an organ donor you can give the gift of life to someone else. It is a wonderful thing. So next time you get your driver's license renewed, sign up to be an organ donor.

On Monday the 24th, 2001, the seventh day after the transplant, I was moved to the Cooperative Care floor. I was in room 4725. Through a lot of research and studies performed by the University of Nebraska, they have found that patients recover faster if the family is the caregiver. The nurses showed Mom how to do vitals and medications. On the 4th floor of the Lied Transplant Center, the care was switched over to the family. The neat thing was that you could go to the 3rd floor for lab draws, and then go to the cafeteria without going outside.

The rooms have one double bed and one single for the patient. There is a separate sitting room for visitors, with a couch that makes into a bed. A large bathroom and shower, lots of handrails, with wheel chair access. On the 25th I was in group therapy and walked everywhere. On the 26th I was discharged from the hospital.

I went to a liver transplant group meeting at 7 p.m. My brother Ken left for home. All that was left was Mom and Dad and I, and no hospital bed. I was still in need of a hospital bed, so I could get up to go to the bathroom. Because of some rule changes, we were not allowed to have a hospital bed on the 7th floor. So there were some baseball player's next door. They went downstairs to our room on the 4th floor at 9 P M. and switched beds. So I have had the same bed for the last few weeks. The hospital beds are adjustable and have handrails to assist me in getting up.

During the middle of the night I started to bleed from my wound. I called the nurse and she said I would have to come down to the 3rd floor, because I now was an outpatient. I went down and the doctor patched me up. But as soon as I got back to my room I started bleeding again from my right side. All night water and blood kept running out of my side, and I thought of Jesus hanging on the cross, with the wound in his side for the forgiveness of my sins. I was so thankful for that experience and felt that God was trying to teach me how forsaken and alone his only begotten son felt, as he was hanging on the cross.

Remember in the previous chapter we were discussing the events of 9-11? The signs of when I was to get my transplant were symbolized by the 3 airplanes striking the towers and Pentagon. But there was a 4th plane that crashes in

Pittsburgh. I could not figure out what was ahead of me, but I was facing another surgery.

Ten days after the transplant I developed a fever of 102.9^0 and was readmitted to the hospital on the 28th. The next day I was at 105^0 fever and then on the 30th I went back into surgery. The doctors thought I had a blockage but after 2 hours of playing football with my liver they sewed me back up. This was a major setback and it was like starting all over again.

The kidneys said, "Let me know when you get done with this nonsense. We will get back to work but we need a little break here first." So the kidneys started resting, because the antibiotics put the kidneys to sleep. And I did 14 days of dialysis, 4 hours each session and one 8-hour session.

I went from 313 pounds to 270 pounds and some days they removed 10 pounds of fluid.

We figured out the amount of blood they drew for labs each day. There was over 1,000 cc total from the daily blood draws. That was like a pitcher of blood. So they started to give me red blood cells to replace the ones they were taking from me. The hemoglobin level was normally around 10. But on the 18th of October it went to 9.4, on the 20th 8.9, on the 21st 7.8, and on the morning of 22nd of October it was 5.2. Guess what, I was leaking like a sieve. I had four ulcers. After 14 units of blood and 2 units of plasma, I was back with the living. The next morning they went in and cauterized the stomach ulcer and it has not leaked since.

I am poured like water, and all my bones are out of joint: my heart is like wax; it is melted in the midst of my bowels.

Psalms 22:14

A poem by Becky Hanson. Encouraging you to sign up to be an organ donor.

Don't Give Up

If you can swallow hard enough to push away the fear,
And say yes to the question that no one wants to hear,
Then you will add a ray of hope when there's nothing left but crying,
And become the "gentle link" between the living and the dying.
I believe that you'll find comfort though your heart has been laid raw.
In offering hope to someone else who prays and waits in awe.
Until it's done you can't know how or whom your words will bless,
But hundreds more will find new life if you answer "yes."

I was not an organ donor. Most people don't give it a second thought. Since my transplant my thinking process is 100% better. I can see better and my hearing has improved. It is amazing how fearfully and wonderfully God has made our body. The liver must work in conjunction with all the other organs in our body to complete the life process of good health. I was taking vitamins and herbs of all kinds before transplant but the disease had progressed too far and nutrition alone was no cure. Exercise, eating lots of fruit and raw vegetables and clean water are the building blocks for a healthy life style. Too much fast food, soda and stress can slowly deteriorate your health. Lot's of sleep and laughter can increase your life span.

My first devotional reading after transplant was on Sept. 26th. The title was Clean, Rebuild and Renew. And be renewed in the spirit of your mind. Ephesians 4:23

I would buy old tools and repair them. I remember an air-operated drill that would not work. I took it apart and found it needed cleaning and some parts replaced. I realized that our lives are a lot like these tools. I would take one apart, and it was basically clean inside. It had a little bit of dirt in it but enough oil to make it operate smoothly. There are people like this who live a clean life and trust God. We all have little specks in our life that need to be dealt with. It seems that God sometimes takes us apart to cleanse us and prepare us for the hard work. Some tools I took apart had oil built up on the inside. Everything was black and dirty, but when cleaned up, the parts were all in good condition. I was able to put it back together, and it worked well. There are people like this who accept Christ, but as they continue on with life, they forget to maintain their spiritual life. Things start to filter in and build up until they can no longer serve God properly. God needs to take them and clean them up so they can once again serve Him. Occasionally when I took a tool apart, I found pieces that were broken and even some shattered. Some peoples' lives are broken and shattered from difficult experiences. Others need to be broken and shattered to get their attention. It doesn't matter which may be the case, God can and wants to replace those pieces so we can serve Him.

St. John chapter 3 verses 1 – 17. This is the account of Nicodemus visiting with Jesus.

1. There was a man of the Pharisees, named Nicodemus, a ruler of the Jews:
2. The same came to Jesus by night, and said unto him, Rabbi we know that thou art a teacher come from God: for no man can do these miracles that thou doest, except God be with him.
3. Jesus answered and said unto him, Verily, verily I say unto thee, Except a man be born again, he cannot see the kingdom of God.

4. Nicodemus saith unto him, How can a man be born when he is old? Can he enter the second time into his mother's womb, and be born?

5. Jesus answered, Verily, verily, I say unto thee, Except a man be born of water and of the Spirit, he cannot enter into the kingdom of God.

6. That which is born of the flesh is flesh; and that which is born of the Spirit is spirit.

7. Marvel not that I said unto thee, Ye must be born again.

8. The wind bloweth where it listeth, and thou hearest the sound therof, but canst not tell whence it cometh, and whither it goeth: so is every one that is born of the Spirit.

9. Nicodemus answered and said unto him, How can these things be?

10. Jesus answered and said unto him, Art thou a master of Israel, and knowest not these things?

11. Verily, verily, I say unto thee, We speak that we do know, and testify that we have seen; and ye receive not our witness.

12. If I have told you earthly things, and ye believe not, how shall ye believe, if I tell you of heavenly things?

13. And no man hath ascended up to heaven, but he that came down from heaven, even the Son of man which is in heaven.

14. And as Moses lifted up the serpent in the wilderness, even so must the Son of man be lifted up:

15. That whosoever believeth in him should not perish, but have eternal life.

16. For God so loved the world, that he gave his only begotten Son, that whosoever believeth in him should not perish, but have everlasting life.

17.For God sent not his Son into the world to condemn the
world; but that the world through him might be saved.

See chapter 10 for more details on how you can experience
rebirth. Every generation needs regeneration.

I had 3 major setbacks in my recovery after the liver
transplant. The doctors would just shake their heads and it
seems that they just couldn't understand why I was still living.
I new the secret. I was being prayed for by thousands of
Christians all around the country.

And the prayer of faith shall save the sick, and the Lord shall raise him up; and if he have committed sins, they shall be forgiven him.

James 5:15

Change

Confess your faults one to another and pray one for another that ye may be healed.

I was very fortunate to have the prayers of literarily hundreds of people from all over the country praying for me. Even school children, people from Florida, Ohio, Indiana, Iowa, Nebraska, Illinois and many more states. I want to express my sincere thanks. On Friday the 14th of September the donor liver was unusable so I was prayed for twice. I was then transplanted the following Tuesday.

I Chronicles 4: 9-10 And Jabez was more honourable than his brethren: and his mother called his name Jabez, saying, Because I bare him with sorrow. And Jabez called on the God of Israel, saying, Oh that thou wouldest bless me indeed, and enlarge my coast, and that thine hand might be with me, and that thou wouldest keep me from evil, that it may not grieve me! And God granted him that which he requested.

Buried in the middle of boring genealogy, is the short biography of Jabez. Because Jabez cried out to God and asked for protection from evil, his prayer was answered. This has been a challenge for me and if you have the faith of Jabez and pray his prayer, many miracles will unfold in your life also.

35

I was at deaths door many times, and the doctors could not understand the miracle of life. Even with all the complications I had, I was not giving up. Remember the 9-11, 4Th plane that crashed in Pennsylvania? I felt that these set backs were God's way of telling me that I need to take charge and if I want to live I must be strong in the faith and trust God to get me through this.

Just as the man in the flood was standing on the roof of his house and a boat came by to rescue him. He said, "God will save me", and refused to get into the boat. Soon the water rose up to the neck of the man as he stood on the top of the chimney. Then a helicopter came along, but he refused help and said, "God will save me." In heaven the man asked God why he did not save him? And God replied, "I sent you a boat and a helicopter."

So you see, we are sometimes blinded by our own self-centered ways and get in a hurry and do not see how we need to take charge and be what God wants us to be. Everyone is made different but we all have been given the same twenty-four hours and it is what we do with our time that can change the outcome of our lives. I used to have pity parties and felt sorry for myself, but nobody came and I decided that was a bad idea. Did you ever have a bad day at work? Did you feel so low you didn't even have to open the front door to your house? You could just slide under the crack. I was so fearful of having a liver transplant that I almost had myself believing that it would never happen.

People would say, "You look so good." I would just say, "I feel fine." But inside I was crying for help. I am sure that you would never do that. I have found that the lack of communication between those you love the most is everyone's problem. My parents would say, "What will the people think?" Isn't that a form of pride?

We need to pray for forgiveness so the peace and joy of Christ can flood into our soul and then trust in the leading of the Lord, in our everyday walk.

Jesus said that when the fig tree flourishes again – when Israel is reborn as a nation – God's kingdom would be close at hand. In light of the certainty of Christ's return, Jesus said his followers should wait with watchfulness for the fulfillment of these signs. Careful Bible students who observe the changes in political, social, and military structures in this generation have witnessed the fulfillment of more prophecies than any other generation since the life of Jesus.

Watch ye therefore, and pray always, that ye may be accounted worthy to escape all these things that shall come to pass, and to stand before the Son of man.   Luke 21:36

Since 9-11 I am reminded of the end times. I think that God is fulfilling end time prophecy right now. The world is getting closer to becoming a one-world government. Next we will have a one-world currency. We are admonished to pray all the time and to be ready for the second coming of Jesus.

Do you believe in miracles? Does prayer really work? After what I have been through I am a firm believer in both. Jesus performed many marvelous miracles of healing when he walked the earth. I think if we truly believe and put our trust in Jesus we can experience the same healing today.

The doctors are practicing medicine and I was the patient. I thought some times, "I am running out of patience with them." Everyone is different. The same night I got my transplant Leo was next door getting his new liver. My surgery lasted 8 hours and his lasted 14. They said when they opened him up his liver exploded and was in very bad shape. My liver was small and looked like a brick. I guess the hardest part of the surgery is taking out the old liver. I had a lady doctor sew in the new liver. After my fever episode they thought I had a blockage in my Portal Vein. They opened me up but found no blockage. Poor Leo. They found a blockage in him and had to open him up too. After the second surgery I was so weak I couldn't even feed myself. Then after each dialysis session my throat got so dry I couldn't talk. I would spend hours sucking on ice cubes to moisten my mouth so I could regain my voice. But praise the Lord all that is in the past now.

Ed was a local Omaha fellow that got his transplant 1 month after mine. He was a happy camper and had his transplant on a Sunday and went home the following Friday. As far as I know he is doing well. Most liver transplant patients have kidney problems and I am no exception. My liver is doing fine but the Prograf anti-rejection medication is slowing down my kidneys. Since my new liver is a foreign organ my body wants to reject it. So I will need to take anti-rejection medication the rest of my life. To monitor the level of medication I am taking a blood test once a week. The results are sent to Omaha and they will call and adjust medication levels as needed.

One of the transplant patients went home after one month but came back because his body was rejecting his new liver. They are changing his medication and I hope he is getting along OK. They perform an average of 2 –3 liver transplants per week at the University Hospital in Omaha. This is a teaching hospital and each day when the doctor would make his rounds there would be 10 – 15 students following him around. After a few years training they would get their surgical or medical degrees.

Now that I have had the prayers of the saints to help me get through the valley, I need to get on with my Christian walk.

And Saul arose from the Earth; and when his eyes were opened, he saw no man: but they led him by the hand, and brought him to Damascus.

Acts 9: 8

The Road to Damascus

We all have choices to make in this life. We can live for the Lord, or we can serve our own selfish interests. Saul was on his way to persecute the disciples of Jesus and was struck down on the road to Damascus. I was forty-nine years old, and God took a big two-by-four, and kept trying to get my attention. He kept hitting me over the head, but I was too stubborn to notice. If we're not reading his word and have sin our lives, God just can't get through to us. Just as Saul was converted to Paul, a new creature in Christ, we too can have this wonderful conversion experience. (See chapter 10.) As I look back now on the past, forty years of wandering in the wilderness, I can see where I have failed in many ways. When times are good, people feel like they don't need God. Just as the people of old built the tower of Babel, God in a single day can confuse the language so that the people scattered across the land. On 9-11, people all across the world looked on in horror, as the two most magnificent man-made towers came crashing down.

Fear is now rampant in our world. Prayer is now much more acceptable and people are going to church more than ever before. The world will never be the same. They say, "Fear knocks at the door, Faith answers it, but there is no one there."

Can you imagine how hard it must have been for Paul to be accepted into the Christian circle? One day he was persecuting Christians, and the next day was converted and a

39

changed man. Just as the liver transplant changed me, I was also changed in my heart. God was very real to me and I want to live for him. We know, just as Paul was persecuted, thrown in jail, and suffered for Christ, we must all be willing to walk closer to Christ, and when there are only one set of footprints in the sand, we know that is when Jesus was there to carry us through the valleys of life.

So how can we have a closer walk with Christ? We need to understand the character qualities that Jesus talks about in his word. Every conflict in life can be traced to the misapplication or neglect of one or more character qualities. The conflicts that a wife has because of her circumstances may be traced to the need for contentment, gratefulness, or joyfulness. If we as husbands do not build up the wife, she may develop low self-esteem and act negatively toward us. A father who is harsh toward his family would need to practice the qualities of patience, gentleness, wisdom, flexibility, humility, self-control, and genuine love. Every character quality also needs balancing qualities. For example, flexibility must be balanced with responsibility and decisiveness; attentiveness needs to be practiced with alertness and discernment.

What is good character? Character is the inward motivation to do what is right according to the highest standards of behavior in every situation. Character is the wise response to the pressure of a difficult situation and what we do when we think that no one is watching. It is the predictor of good behavior. Understanding character explains why things happen to us, because all things work together for good to conform us to the character of Christ.

All things are for our good, even unpleasant circumstances. "And we know that all things work together for

40

good to them that love God, to them who are the called according to his purpose." Romans 8: 28

All character is personified in Christ. Therefore, to have His power in us is to have all we need for character development. "That Christ may dwell in your hearts by faith; that ye, being rooted and grounded in love, May be able to comprehend with all saints what is the breadth, and length, and depth, and height; And to know the love of Christ, which passeth knowledge, that ye might be filled with all the fullness of God. Now unto him that is able to do exceeding abundantly above all that we ask or think, according to the power that worketh in us." Ephesians 3: 17-20

Success is determined by relationships, and relationships are determined by character. Vital relationships require getting along with ourselves, with our families. With our life partner, with our children, with our businesses, churches, communities, and most importantly, with God. True success involves proper relationships in all these areas. If a man is successful in business but a failure in his marriage and family, he cannot be identified as truly successful.

The rest of chapter six lists forty-nine character qualities that are expressions of genuine love. When understood these qualities will produce true success. Remember I had 49 staples to hold my incision together and I am 49 years old!

LOVE - Selfishness
Love is giving to the basic needs of others so
that their authorities get the credit, God gets the
glory, and we have the joy of eternal rewards.

ALERTNESS - Carelessness
Alertness is exercising my physical and

spiritual senses to recognize the dangers that
could diminish the resources entrusted to me.

ATTENTIVENESS – Distraction
Attentiveness is giving a "hearing
heart" to people or projects
that need our concentration.

AVAILABILITY – Self-Centeredness
Availability is simplifying our daily needs
so we are ready and able to serve
those whom God brings to us.

BOLDNESS – Fearfulness
Boldness is welcoming any suffering that comes
from doing what is right, because it will
produce a greater power of love.

CAUTIOUSNESS – Rashness
Cautiousness is planning for the success
of a venture by following the ways of
God rather than my natural inclinations.

COMPASSION – Indifference
Compassion is responding to a
deep need with a longing to do
whatever is necessary to meet it.

CONTENTMENT – Covetousness
Contentment is realizing that God has
already provided everything I need for
my present and future happiness.

CREATIVITY – Underachievement
Creativity is cultivating wise thoughts,
prudent words, and skillful actions
to carry out God's will.

DECISIVENESS – Double-Mindedness
Decisiveness is choosing to do
what is right based on accurate facts,
wise counsel, and clearly defined goals.

DEFERENCE – Offensiveness
Deference is putting
the welfare of others
ahead of our own personal pleasures.

DEPENDABILITY – Inconsistency
Dependability is purposing
in our hearts to do the
will of God whatever the cost.

DETERMINATION – Faintheartedness
Determination is looking at
insurmountable obstacles as opportunities
to cry out for God's supernatural intervention.

DILIGENCE – Slothfulness
Diligence is accepting each task as a special
assignment from the Lord and using all my
energies to do it quickly and skillfully.

DISCERNMENT – Judgment
Discernment is the ability to distinguish

between what is good and what is evil,
in order to make wise decisions.

DISCRETION – Simple-Mindedness
Discretion is using wisdom to avoid
damaging attitudes, words, and actions
and to give insightful counsel.

ENDURANCE – Discouragement
Endurance is experiencing
the power of God's love by
rejoicing in trials and tribulations

ENTHUSIASM – Apathy
Enthusiasm is God's energy
in my spirit expressing itself through
my mind, will, and emotions.

FAITH – Unbelief
Faith is recognizing God's will
in a given matter and acting upon it.

FLEXIBILITY – Resistance
Flexibility is not setting my affections on
plans or places that could be changed
by those whom I am serving.

FORGIVENESS – Bitterness
Forgiveness is responding to offenders
so that the power of God's love
through me can heal them.

GENEROSITY – Stinginess
Generosity is demonstrating the nature
of God by wisely reinvesting the
resources the He has entrusted to us.

GENTLENESS – Harshness
Gentleness is supporting others during
their times of weakness so that they can
achieve their full potential in the Lord.

GRATEFULNESS – Murmuring
Gratefulness is expressing sincere
appreciation to God and to others for the
ways that they have benefited my life.

HONOR – Disrespect
Honor is humbling myself in the presence
of a God-given authority and expressing
my devotion with an appropriate gift.

HOSPITALITY – Unfriendliness
Hospitality is using
what God has given to us to
demonstrate His love for others.

HUMILITY – Pride
Humility is recognizing and acknowledging
my total dependence upon the Lord
and seeking His will for every decision.

INITIATIVE – Idleness
Initiative is acting on the rhemas

that God gives to us in His Word.

JOYFULNESS – Self-Pity
Joyfulness is the bright spirit and radiant
countenance that comes by being
in full fellowship with the Lord.

JUSTICE – Fairness
Justice is carrying out wise
judgments based on the laws and
character of God.

LOYALTY – Infidelity
Loyalty is the bonding of individuals
in a long-term commitment of
sacrificial support and defense.

MEEKNESS – Anger
Meekness is yielding our rights
to God so He can demonstrate
His peace and power through us.

OBEDIENCE – Willfulness
Obedience is freedom to be creative
under the protection of divinely
appointed authorities.

ORDERLINESS – Confusion
Orderliness is keeping
everything that is under our jurisdiction
neat, clean, functional, and in its proper place.

PATIENCE – Restlessness
Patience is welcoming trials and
tribulations as friends and allowing
them to perfect our character.

PERSUASIVENESS – Contentiousness
Persuasiveness is convincing others to
follow God's ways because of how His ways
are working in our lives.

PUNCTUALITY –Tardiness
Punctuality is demonstrating the worth
of people and time by arriving for
appointments before they begin.

RECOURCEFULNESS – Wastefulness
Resourcefulness is increasing
assets by seeing value in what
others overlook or discard.

RESPONSIBILITY – Unreliability
Responsibility is knowing and doing what God
and others are expecting of me.

SECURITY – Anxiety
Security is knowing that God will never leave
us nor forsake us and that whatever we give
to Him will become an eternal treasure.

SELF-CONTROL – Self-Indulgence
Self-control is the power of the Holy Spirit that
results from passing the tests of the Spirit.

SENSITIVITY – Callousness
Sensitivity is being aware of the pain
in others because of the healing we
have received from God for similar hurts.

SINCERITY – Hypocrisy
Sincerity is being as genuine
on the inside as we appear
to be on the outside.

THOROUGHNESS – Incompleteness
Thoroughness is carrying out each task
in preparation for God's personal
inspection and approval

THRIFTINESS – Extravagance
Thriftiness is multiplying my resources
through wise investments so I have
more to give back to God.

TOLERANCE – Condemnation
Tolerance is making allowances for those
who lack wisdom or maturity and praying
that they will see and follow God's ways.

TRUTHFULNESS – Deception
Truthfulness is communicating
by life and word what is
genuine and accurate.

VIRTUE – Weakness
Virtue is the power of a life
that is in harmony with the
holy standards of God.

WISDOM – Foolishness
Wisdom is seeing the hand of God
in every experience of life.

These preceding forty-nine positive and negative character traits were used by permission from:

The Institute in Basic Life Principles, Inc.
Box One
Oak Brook, Il. 60522-3001
Phone: (630) 323-9800
For more information and further study ask them for their new book entitled:
THE POWER FOR TRUE SUCCESS
How to build character in your life

Divorce is a terrible thing, and as a Mennonite, I didn't think it would ever happen to me. After 22 years of marriage the sky started to fall!

And unto the married I command, yet not I but the Lord, Let not the wife depart from her husband. But and if she depart, let her remain unmarried, or be reconciled to her husband: and let not the husband put away his wife

I Corinthians, 7:10,11

What not to Do!

The lawyers were arguing. The judge was indifferent. After all to them it was just another day in divorce court. I found out the hard way. The only people who win in divorce court are the lawyers. At $150.00 an hour the more you resist the more you loose.

So how in the world did two people get in so much trouble?

It all started back in June of 1973. After our honeymoon in the Bahamas, we settled down to a new life together. Sarah my wife was a very conscientious lady and would go out of her way to give back fifty cents to the grocery store clerk if they made a mistake.

Our first argument was over how much bacon costs and we decided to do without! As time went on we wanted to start a family. Her dream was to have a lot of babies. We would baby sit for her sisters and her friends. Due to health problems we found out that we could not have children of our own. So we decided to adopt and even went through a foster child program.

But how did we end up in divorce court? As a Mennonite couple we do not believe in divorce and are looked upon with distain. People thought there must be something wrong with me. I was a trustee in church and on the building committee. I was also Sunday School Superintendent for many years. After the divorce I was not allowed to take part in any church office. I also was not allowed to partake in communion. It was a very depressing time. Our faith taught us it was wrong to get remarried, so I just resigned to live a single life.

One thing that women like, is to be told that you love them. Don't do what I did. The saying goes; "If I stop loving you, I will let you know." Women like flowers and phone calls in the middle of the day just to see how their day is going. I would get home from work and having already said my 500 words for the day was finished talking and looking for some peace and quiet. And then she would want to talk, I would say "I'm finished listening," but she would go on and on and on and on.

I hate to see when other men criticize their spouse in a group setting. There is no such thing as constructive criticism. It is very destructive. It wears down the self-esteem in a wife.

The husband is to be under the umbrella of God. If the husband is in total submission to God, as the Church is, then the wife needs to be under the authority of the husband. Then the children, in that order. If the order is broken then the marriage is doomed. New families are coming off the assembly line every day. Nothing is more inspirational than the uniting of two unique personalities in a marital commitment that will last for a lifetime, with God's help. Who can comprehend this mysterious bonding that enables a man and woman to withstand the many storms of life and remain best friends to the end of their lives together? This phenomenon is so remarkable that the Apostle Paul, under divine inspiration, chose it to symbolize the unfathomable bond of love between Jesus Christ and His bride, the church. Unfortunately, a depressing number of today's marriages end on a less inspirational note. Indeed, Western nations are witnessing a continuing epidemic of dysfunctional relationships.

The agony inflicted by divorce cannot be overstated. The standard approach to marriage counseling is to teach husbands and wives how to revitalize unhealthy relationships and help them work through their conflicts. Unfortunately, such advice assumes that both parties are equally motivated to work on their problems. That is rarely the case. We went to Christian counselors and spent lots of money to no avail because neither one of us was willing to acknowledge our faults. Typically, when a marriage is unraveling, there is one partner who is less concerned about the prospect of divorce, while the other is terrified by it. He or she may have decided already that the relationship is over. It has been my observation that the way the committed partner responds at that vital juncture will determine whether the marriage will survive or succumb.

Only those who have been rejected by a beloved spouse can fully comprehend the tidal wave of pain that crashes into one's life when a relationship ends. Nothing else matters. There are no consoling thoughts. The future is without interest or hope. Emotions swing wildly from despair to acceptance and back again. If one word must be selected to describe the entire experience, it would be something equivalent to panic. Just as a drowning person exhausts himself or herself in a desperate attempt to grasp anything that floats, a rejected partner typically tries to grab and hold the one who is leaving. This panic then leads to appeasement, which destroys what is left of the marriage. The critical element is the way a husband or wife begins to devalue the other and their lives together. It is a subtle thing at first, often occurring without either partner being aware of the slippage. But as time passes, one individual begins to feel trapped in a relationship with someone he or she no longer respects. Now we begin to see why groveling, crying and pleading by a panic-stricken partner tend to drive the claustrophobic partner even farther away. The more he or she struggles to gain a measure of freedom (or even secure a little breathing room), the more desperately the rejected spouse attempts to hang on. Perhaps it is now apparent where the present line of reasoning is leading us. If there is hope for dying marriages, and I certainly believe there is, then it is likely to be found in the reconstruction of respect between warring husbands and wives. That requires the vulnerable spouse to open the cage door and let the trapped partner out! All the techniques of containment must end immediately, including manipulative grief, anger, guilt and appeasement. Begging, pleading, crying, hand-wringing and playing the role of the doormat are equally destructive. There may be a time and place for strong feelings to be expressed, and there may be an occasion for quiet tolerance. But these responses must not be used as persuasive devices to hold the drifting partner against his or her will. I'm sure you would not have dreamed of using these coercive methods to convince your husband or wife to marry you during your dating days. You had to lure, attract, charm and encourage him or her. Coercing and manipulating a potential marriage partner is like high-pressure tactics by a used car salesman. What do you think he would accomplish by telling a potential customer through his tears, "Oh, please, buy this car! I need the money so badly and I've only had two sales so far this week." When one has fallen in love with an eligible partner, he attempts to "sell himself" to the other. But like the salesman, he must not deprive the buyer of free choice in the matter. Instead, he must convince the customer that the purchase is in his own interest. If a person would not buy an automobile to ease the pain of a salesman, how much more unlikely is he to devote his entire being to someone he doesn't love, simply for benevolent reasons? None of us is that unselfish. Ideally, we are permitted by God to select only one person in the course of a lifetime, and few are willing to squander that one shot on someone we merely pity! In fact, it is very difficult to love another person romantically and pity him or her at the same time. If begging and pleading are ineffective methods of attracting a member of the opposite sex during the dating days, why do victims of bad marriages use the same groveling techniques to hold a drifting spouse? They only increase the depth of disrespect by the one who is escaping. To a person like me, who expected to marry only once and to remain committed for life, it is a severe shock to see our relationship begin to unravel. Nevertheless, I have done some intense soul-searching, and I now realize that I have been attempting to hold you against your will. That simply can't be done. As I reflect on our courtship and early years together, I'm reminded that you married me of your own free choice. It was a decision you made without pressure from me. Now you say you want out of the marriage, and obviously, I have to let you go. I'm aware that I can no more force you to stay today than I could have made you marry me in 1973. You are free to go. If you never call me again, then I will accept your decision. I admit that this entire experience has been painful, but I'm going to make it. The Lord has been with me thus far and He'll go with me in the future. You and I had some wonderful times together. "But there must be a catch," she thinks. "It's too good to be true. Talk is cheap. This is just another trick to win me back. In a week or two she'll be crying on the phone again, begging me to come home. She's really weak, you know, and she'll crack under pressure."

It is my strongest recommendation that you, the rejected person, prove your partner wrong in this expectation. Let her marvel at your self-control in coming weeks. Only the passage of time will convince her that you are serious—that she is actually free. But one thing is certain: She will be watching for signs of weakness or strength. The vestiges of respect hang in the balance. If the more vulnerable spouse passes the initial test and convinces the partner that her freedom is secure, some interesting changes begin to occur in their relationship. Please understand that every situation is unique and I am merely describing typical reactions, but these developments are extremely common in families I have seen. Most of the exceptions represent variations on the same theme. Three distinct consequences can be anticipated when a previously "grabby" lover begins to let go of the cool spouse:

1. The trapped partner no longer feels it necessary to fight off the other, and their relationship improves. It is not that the love affair is rekindled, necessarily, but the strain between the two partners is often eased.

2. As the cool spouse begins to feel free again, the question she has been asking herself changes. After wondering for weeks or months, "How can I get out of this mess?" she now asks, "Do I really want to go?" Just knowing that she can have her way often makes her less anxious to achieve it. Sometimes it turns her around 180 degrees and brings her back home!

3. The third change occurs not in the mind of the cool spouse but in the mind of the vulnerable one. Incredibly, he or she feels better—somehow more in control of the situation. There is no greater agony than journeying

through a vale of tears, waiting in vain for the phone to
ring or for a miracle to occur.

Instead, the person has begun to respect himself or herself and
to receive small evidences of respect in return. Even though it is
difficult to let go once and for all, there are ample rewards for
doing so. One of those advantages involves the feeling that he
or she has a plan—a program—a definite course of action to
follow. That is infinitely more comfortable than experiencing
the utter despair of powerlessness that the victim felt before.
And little by little, the healing process begins. This
recommendation is consistent with the Apostle Paul's writings
in 1 Corinthians 7:15: "But if the unbeliever leaves, let him do
so. A believing man or woman is not bound in such
circumstances. God has called us to live in peace" (NIV). Paul
is not authorizing the rejected spouse to initiate a divorce in
these instances. He is, rather, instructing a man or woman to
release the marital partner when he or she is determined to
depart. The advice I have offered today is an expression of that
scripture. I hope it will be helpful to those who have been
struggling to keep a troubled marriage alive. In a broader sense,
the principles I have described are not only relevant to husbands
and wives in a time of crisis; they are applicable to healthier
marriages, too. Indeed, I wish they could be taught to every
engaged or newlywed couple in the morning of their lives
together. There would be fewer bitter divorces if young
husbands and wives knew how to draw their drifting partners
toward them, rather than relentlessly driving them away.
Respect, you see, is not only vital to rebuilding broken
marriages, but to preserving healthy relationships day by day.
Genuine insights into human behavior are not everyday
occurrences—at least not for me. Indeed, if one stumbles onto
two or three fundamental principles in the course of a lifetime,

he or she, has done well. Do they always preserve dysfunctional marriages? Of course not. No one can make that promise. But even in cases where the spark of love has died, the principle of self-respect in the face of rejection holds true. The alternative is usually despair. Though I haven't emphasized the role of prayer in the preservation of a troubled family, I'm sure you know that it is the key to everything. The institution of marriage was God's design, and He has promised to answer those who ask for His healing touch. Still, it helps to understand your spouse as you seek to restore what God has "joined together.

Since neither of us have remarried we are working on reconciling our marriage. With God all things are possible but we must be willing to give and take and be submissive one to another.

We have some neighbors in Illinois that were Emergency Ambulance Technicians, part time. Several years ago the husband was on the roof with a water hose cleaning out the gutters. He told his wife that she should check on him in a little while. But she got busy and was on the phone with a friend. Sure enough the water hose got caught on the ladder and it fell to the ground. Now it was getting colder and the husband was stranded on the roof without a coat. He used his cell phone to call his wife but the phone was busy. He yelled at the top of his lungs but his wife did not hear him. Finally, as he was freezing he called the rescue squad to come and get him. His fellow members of the EMT team were quite amused, as the husband climbed down from the roof.

Now I am sure we have all been in situations that would make a grown man cry. It is how we handle the situation that is important.

The Bible says to not go to bed angry but to ask for forgiveness and to make restitution. By now you must be thinking, I am making up this story but every word is true! Just as Job, in the Old Testament, was tried for his faith God was preparing me for a higher calling.

Do not be discouraged!

Having predestinated us unto the adoption of children by Jesus Christ to himself, according to the good pleasure of his will.

Ephesians 1:5

Adoption

We were vacationing in Ohio back in 1981 when we got a call from our Pastor in Florida. There was a young woman from Plano Texas who was looking for a Mennonite couple to adopt her two baby boys. One was 9 months old, the other, almost 2 years old. She could no longer care for them. Would we be interested? Wow! We were in shock. Knowing how much my wife wanted children, I said, "Yes," first and we went to Texas on blind faith, not knowing what the boys even looked like. That is when Mark and Mike, who have different fathers but same mother, came into our lives.

We had a wonderful time with the boys, but noticed that the older one had emotional problems. Mark never did bond with us. Both boys had a very difficult time in school. Mark would run away from school and we were always looking for him all over the neighborhood. My wife finally home schooled both boys because of their problems. We even sent them to a private Christian Day School, but to no avail. We even tried Ritalin and that didn't seem to help. They were both diagnosed with Attention Deficit Disorder. I think that is a bunch of hobble gook! At age 10 he would get on his bike and be gone for hours. One time we got a call from the security guard at K-Mart. "Do you have a son with blond hair?" Yes we do! When

59

we went to pick him up he had on two right side only, new tennis shoes. It seems they only had the right foot shoes on display. We made him apologize and took him home. Later that summer the fire department called and said someone saw him start a fire in the woods. We knew he was getting out of hand and sent him to live with my brother and his family for six months. But the problems remained and finally his biological father agreed to raise him. But like a bad penny would always come back. Next he lived with his mother who was now living in Ohio. He spent most of his youth in juvenile detention and then in a group home. He just could never quite get it together. He now has contracted Hepatitis and is in a Georgia prison. Pray for him that he would see that the path he has chosen in life would lead to destruction. Mike the younger son is now attending church and wants to get married. He just turned 21 and is finally growing up.

It is interesting, now that Mike is getting older, how he thinks his Dad is smarter, than he used to be. He even calls to ask for advice, now and then.

There is a very well thought of Amish couple that also could not have children of their own. They adopted two children, a boy and a girl. They too have experienced much heartache. The girl married and had several children. Then her husband left her. One evening her young son was biking on the road and was killed by an oncoming car. A year later the other adopted son was drinking and flipped his car in a ditch and was also killed. His name was Ernie. I don't know why some adoptions work and others fail miserably. It seems that there is a feeling of rejection in the children. Why would my real parents give me away?

We can also see that many adoptions work very well. We have told our boys how special they are, since we chose them. Other boy's and girls have no choice in parents. Of the approximate two million pregnancies that occur among unmarried women each year, only one percent choose adoption. Despite dramatic changes in adoption over the past 10 to 15 years, a shadow still hangs over the adoption process. For most, thoughts of adoption remain mired in images of the past when babies were whisked away before their mothers had a chance to see them. For others, recent stories of fully open adoptions and high-profile court cases where children were removed from adoptive families have laced adoption with frightening uncertainties.

People don't see adoption as the sacrificial love it really is. Women are not going to choose adoption until we change the heart of the nation. And I think it has to start with us Christians.

The truth is far from these extremes. Most adoption agencies, especially Christian ones, offer a loving, supportive process for the woman who chooses to place her baby with another family. As a result, many women are learning how to turn their crisis into a blessing.

We are all adopted into the family of God.

For ye were sometimes darkness, but now are ye light in the Lord: walk as children of light. Ephesians 5:8

If only we could all have a second chance in life. What would you do differently?

A Second Chance

But Noah found grace in the eyes of the Lord.

Genesis 6:8

Grace

The world is wicked and the devil has many snares out to lull the Christian to sleep. Jealousy, pride, gossip and slander of others is common among our churches. Why are there so many pastors burning out? It seems like there is something missing.

As a liver transplant patient, I will have to take anti-rejection drugs the rest of my life. I need to keep my body's immune system low, so the new liver will not be noticed by my body, as a foreign organ.

If you think about it the anti-rejection in a Christian life is LOVE! I Corinthians 13:13 says, "And now abideth faith, hope, charity, these three; but the greatest of these is charity."

Noah was found righteous and was saved from the flood, for a new beginning.

God saw fit to give me another chance in life. I am a new creature in Christ. I hope you can be encouraged by reading this book and would pass it on as a way of spreading the Gospel.

Since I am a High School dropout, I am sure God can use your talents much more than my feeble efforts. Go write your own story. Tell the world honestly how you feel! Miracles do happen even today. Just, as Jesus healed the people, 2000 years ago, His angels are watching over each one of us. God says in His Word that he knows the number of hairs on each of our heads. He is all knowing and present every where. It is more than us mere mortals can comprehend.

I was driving a semi-truck from Illinois to Grand Rapids Michigan, the last several years. Some times I would not get much sleep. I would leave at midnight from Champaign and get to Chicago around 3 A.M. I recall waking up in Chicago in time to take I 80 E to the tollbooth. I did not remember anything for 200 miles. I saw many accidents and because God was watching over me, I did not have one accident. I should not have been driving at all. I was losing a lot of blood and was very anemic. That condition I found out later, according to my doctor, causes poor reaction time and makes me very sleepy. On my days off, I would sometimes sleep all day.

Before transplant I had trouble seeing and hearing. My mind was slow and to try to think would be an exhaustive effort. I would always be extremely tired. I was taking several prescription drugs for arthritis and water retention. I now no longer need to take those. I would always get cold sores and fever blisters. Every time I would get sick with a fever and chills, I would develop fever blisters a few days later. I have not had one fever blister since transplant, even though I had 105 degrees fever.

After transplant I decided to put this book together. I could see without my glasses and my hearing is perfect. I can think clearer than ever. I have more to say than people want to hear! Ha! Ha!

Just as God gave me a second chance physically and spiritually, I would like you to read the last chapter and make a decision to live for the Lord, before it is forever too late.

In the hospital, we have heard of many that did not recover from surgery. Some people just gave up. I was a fighter and strong willed. I wanted to live. At 49, I have a mission now to help others through my experience. The Bible is very clear on teaching others. Knowledge is a stepping-stone to wisdom.

So why would anyone want to change their lifestyle and lose their status quo?

"The wicked shall be turned into hell, and all nations that forget God." Psalm 9:17

Since 9-11 there seems to be a renewed interest in reading of the Bible. Church attendance is at an all time high. But how soon will we forget? Just as the children of Israel forgot about the miraculous crossing of the river out of Egypt, they started to complain and were soon worshiping idols.

Let us not make that new house, car, clothes and big bank account our idol. Give of your tithes and offerings to the Lord. If we give everything to God we don't have to worry about it. The rich man goes to sleep at night worried that someone will steal his possessions. The poor man or true Christian that has given all over to the Lord, can sleep like a baby because he knows that in the morning all his needs will be taken care of.

It is worth it all!

To an inheritance incorruptible, and undefiled, and that fadeth not away, reserved in heaven for you, Who are kept by the power of God through faith unto salvation ready to be revealed in the last time.

I Peter 1: 4,5

Heaven

In harmony with a gracious loving heavenly Father, we should reserve for the last a subject, which, next to God, is the most important – HEAVEN.

We are blessed with many unmerited favors, but the best of human life is mixed with disappointments. Over yonder is a world unmixed with the sorrows of earth, abounding in endless bliss and glory of which the most blissful things of earth are but temporary foretastes.

On my bedroom wall there is a plaque that has some very profound words written, to direct my every day walk.

Rules For Today

Do nothing that you
Would not like to be doing
When Jesus Comes

Go to no place where you
Would not like to be found
When Jesus Comes

Say nothing that you
Would not like to be saying
When Jesus Comes

Sometimes suffering comes to test our faith in Almighty God. The Bible tells the story of a man named Job, the greatest man of the East. To prove Job's unswerving faith in God, God allowed Satan to strip Job of all he owned-his possessions and his children-in one cataclysmic day. But Job was triumphant in suffering. Summarizing that tragic day, Job declared, "The Lord gave, and the Lord hath taken away; Blessed be the name of the Lord" (Job 1:21). His faith in God remained intact. He had passed the test. Is God testing my faith in Him? Sometimes suffering comes to increase our faith. When all goes well, we tend to trust in material things for our security. On 9-11 many people across the world realized that what they though was secure was no longer secure. Terror could strike anywhere at any time. Much of society is now praying. That is a beautiful start to recovery from the chaos of destruction.

As you humbly yield your life to God, He will hear from heaven and will forgive your sin, bringing healing and HOPE to your soul. God's Spirit will fill you, and your life will radiate the fruit of the Spirit. "The fruit of the Spirit is love, joy, peace, longsuffering, gentleness, goodness, faith, meekness, temperance" (Galatians 5:22-23).

This healing peace from God is a calm assurance that rests the hearts of those who surrender their wills to God's will.

So how do we receive the "Gift of Eternal Life?"

We hear a lot about being born again. Billy Graham talks about it. The Bible says something about it also, It says, "Except a man be 'born again,' he cannot see the Kingdom of God." Being "born again" means a brand new life, receiving the gift of eternal life by trusting in Jesus Christ alone for your salvation. You can receive Jesus Christ as your Lord and Savior and invite Him to sit on the throne of your life and immediately you have the gift of eternal life. You receive joy; peace, happiness and all your sins are forgiven. Your name is written in God's book of life.

I know we all have our good points. I go to Church every Sunday, and sometimes I even go Wednesday evening to prayer meeting. But the things you do and the things you don't do are wonderful, but that doesn't make you a Christian. You just don't get to heaven by the good life you lead.

We are all born sinners. John 8:44 says, "Ye are of your father, the devil." That's a pretty strong scripture, but do you know who said that? Jesus Christ. Who did he say it to? The religious people of that day. Romans 5:12 says, "For by one man, sin entered the world and death by sin, so death passed upon all men, for all have sinned."

If we could get to Heaven by being good, Christ wouldn't have had to die on the cross. The best we can do is still not good enough. Isaiah 64 says, "Our righteousness is as filthy rags."

Marvel not that I say unto you, you must be born again. There is no eternal life in good works. Eternal life is in a person, Jesus Christ.

The Bible says, "Therefore if any man be in Christ, he is a new creature, old things pass away, behold all things become new."

How do you know when you have received the gift of eternal life? God's Word says, "This is the record, that God has given to us eternal life and this life is in His Son. He that hath the Son of God hath life and he that hath not the Son of God hath not life." His spirit bears witness with your spirit.

Would you like to pray right now and receive the Gift of eternal life by trusting in Jesus Christ alone for your salvation?

Here is the prayer:

AN INVITATION

Right now, in the presence of God, I acknowledge my own emptiness and sin. I truly believe that God loves me and that His Son, Jesus Christ, died to put away my sins and arose again. Believing this with all my heart.

I now receive the gift of eternal life by trusting in Jesus Christ alone for my salvation. As Christ helps me, I shall confess before all.

Signed:_____

Date:_____

Revelation 22: 12-14

And behold, I come quickly and my reward is with me, to give every man according as his work shall be. I am Alpha and Omega, the beginning and the end, the first and the last. Blessed are they that do his commandments, that they may have right to the tree of Life, and may enter in through the gates into the city.

Nearly two thousand years ago the heavenly host proclaimed the gory of God, saying, "Glory to God in the highest, and on earth peace, good will toward men." With an eye of faith we can see the King upon His throne surrounded by a great throng of saints and angels. We think of the glory, which surrounds the throne of God in heaven; of the majesty and power and goodness and purity and wisdom and dominion of the mighty King of kings and Lord of lords; of the saints of God and holy angels in unnumbered millions praising and glorifying His high and holy name; of the ransomed hosts of God singing the song of everlasting deliverance; of the immeasurable space, the indescribable beauty, the matchless purity, and the perfect bliss of those whose happy lot it will be to share in this wondrous glory; of the heavenly light that far outshines the brightness of the noonday sun, the Lamb of God being the light thereof. Glorious and wonderful, both the Throne and He that sitteth thereon - happy the lot of those whose blissful privilege it will be to have a part in His never ending reign.

We have reached the portals. The way that leads to the pearly gates has been traveled. We hear the blessed invitation, "Come, ye blessed of my Father, inherit the Kingdom." That glorious land, so vividly described in Scripture and so ardently longed for by every child of God, is now in plain sight. How wonderful that the grace of God has made us heirs of glory.

Then we think of the endless ages in which we shall be in is hallowed presence, in the fellowship of saints and angels, in the fullness of bliss and glory in the land where farewell tears are never shed and sorrows never come. Meditating upon these things, may we breathe a prayer to God that He may grant us long lives and healthy bodies here, thus extending the time of opportunities to give this vision of a blessed eternity to as many people as are willing to receive the message of salvation. Yes, we want to go home, and long for the time to come when we may – but not until we have done all that lies within our power to do to the end that others also may set their faces heavenward, and set their affections upon this eternal home and make that the goal of their lives.

As I lay down my pen, it is with the sincere prayer that the blessed hope of the "glorious appearing of the great God and our Saviour Jesus Christ," who will come to take His own to be with him forevermore, and that we may all dedicate ourselves anew to the great cause of carrying this Gospel of eternal salvation to the ends of the earth. With earth as our stepping-stone, we can take advantage of our opportunity to reach our GOAL – HEAVEN.

Poem

"To remember me"

The day will come when my body will lie upon a white sheet neatly tucked under four corners of a mattress located in a hospital busily occupied with the living and the dying. At a certain moment a doctor will determine that my brain has ceased to function and that, for all intents and purposes, my life has ended. When that happens, do not attempt to instill artificial life into my body by the use of a machine. And don't call this my deathbed. Let it be called the bed of life, and let my body be taken from it to help others lead fuller lives.

Give my sight to the man who has never seen a sunrise, a baby's face or love in the eyes of a woman.

Give my heart to a person whose own heart has caused nothing but endless days of pain.

Give my blood to the teenager who was pulled from the wreckage of his car, so that he might live to see his grandchildren play.

Give my kidneys to one who depends on a machine to exist from week to week.

Take my bones, every muscle, every fiber and nerve in my body and find a way to make a crippled child walk.

Explore every corner of my brain. Take my cells, if necessary, and let them grow so that, someday a speechless boy will shout at the crack of a bat and a deaf girl will hear the sound of rain against her window.

If you must bury something, let it be my faults, my weaknesses and all prejudice against my fellow man.

Give my sins to the devil. Give my soul to God.

If, by chance, you wish to remember me, do it with a kind deed or word to someone who needs you.

If you do all I have asked, I will live forever.

~ *By Robert N. Test*

TRANSPLANT STATISTICS

Transplant Waiting List			2000 Organ Transplants	
National		**78,241**	Kidney	13,372
Nebraska		**424**	Liver	4,954
	NE	National	Pancreas alone	435
Kidney	178	49,923	Kidney-Pancreas	911
Kidney-Pancreas	25	2,490	Intestine	79
Liver	129	18,411	Heart	2,198
Heart	30	4,181	Heart-lung	48
Lung	24	3,776	Lung	956
Heart-Lung	0	212		
Pancreas	12	1,145	**2000 Organ Donors**	
Pancreas Islets	0	248	National	5,984
Small Bowel	26	179	Nebraska	32
September 2001				

NEBRASKA TRANSPLANT HOSPITALS

Nebraska Health System in Omaha — Heart, Lung, Liver, Small Bowel, Kidney and Pancreas

Bryan LGH Hospital in Lincoln - Heart & Lung

ORGAN AND TISSUE DONATION SAVES LIVES

* One person who decides to be an organ and tissue donor can save the lives of up to 8 people through organ donation and improve the quality of life for over 50 people through tissue donation.

EYE & TISSUE DONATION IMPROVES QUALITY OF LIFE

* Tissues used for transplant include: eyes, heart valves, skin, ligaments, tendons, bone & major blood vessels.
* Over 56 people in Nebraska are waiting for cornea transplants.
* 500,000 tissue transplants are performed each year in the U.S.
* 80% of patients with cancerous bone tumors keep their limbs due to revolutionary bone and tissue transplant techniques.

Organ & Tissue Donation

For More Information, Please Contact
The Organ and Tissue Donor Task Force of Nebraska
1-800-718-LIFE
402-559-3788 in Omaha

Organ Donation

A wide variety of organizations provide information on organ and tissue donations.

The American Association of Tissue Banks, (703) 827- 9582, http://www.aatb.org

The American Red Cross Tissue Services, (888) 4-TISSUE, http://www.redcross.org/tissue

The Association of Organ Procurement Organizations, (703) 573-2676, http://www.aopo.org

The Coalition on Donation, (800) 355-SHARE, http://www.shareyourlife.org/

The Division of Transplantation at the Department of Health and Human Services, (301) 443-7577, http://www.hrsa.gov/osp/dot/

The James Redford Institute for Transplant Awareness, (310) 441-4906, http://www.jrifilms.org

The National Kidney Foundation, (800) 622-9010, http://www.kidney.org

The North American Transplant Coordinators Organization, (913) 492-3600, http://www.natco1.org

Nebraska Health System 1-800-95-ORGAN nebraskatransplant.org

TransWeb, http://www.transweb.org

The United Network for Organ Sharing, (800) 292-9547, http://www.unos.org